Reflection of Life

DR. JOYCE F. PULLEN

Copyright © 2022 Dr. Joyce F. Pullen

All rights reserved. No part of this book may be reproduced in any form without permission in writing from the publisher, except in the case of brief quotations embodied in critical articles or reviews. Unauthorized reproduction of any part of this work is illegal and is punishable by law.

The author and publisher shall have neither liability nor responsibility for anyone with respect to any loss or damage caused directly or indirectly, by the information contained in this book.

ISBN: 978-1-950861-67-5

Photos Used for Poetry: pixabay.com

Scripture references are used with permission from Zondervan via Biblegateway.com

Printed in the United States of America
10 9 8 7 6 5 4 3 2

Acknowledgements

I give my Lord and Savior all the Praise, Honor and Glory for who He is in my life. I thank God for giving me the strength and energy to finish what He started in the mighty name of Jesus.

Proverb 3:5-6 states, "Trust in the Lord with all thine heart and lean not unto thine own understanding. In all thy ways acknowledge Him and He shall direct thy path."

I thank God for my daughter Akia Rowe Jones and my son Reymundo Highsmith. You both continue to be my inspiration to work hard, and I am blessed to call you, my children. I love you both.

I also thank God for my sister Loretta A. Hilliard who has played, and still plays a major role in my life as my only living sibling. She has truly been a blessing to me. I praise God for her.

I dedicate this book in loving memory of my son

Travis M. Hilliard
11/10/1983 -3/30/2013

A Mother's Cry

When the sun rises, the sun also has to set
But what we need to realize is…. life is not over yet

The pain and the misery have only been taken away
However, the love we have for you will always stay

There's an old saying that states….
Gone too soon
My question is…. what is too soon?

When God gets ready for you to come home, there is nothing we can do because only God knows what is best for you.

It is not over yet
Your life has just begun
Knowing your new life is on hold….Resting
Waiting for God's Only Son

As we know when the sun rises, the sun also has to set
We still need to realize that it is not over yet

Table of Contents

Introduction 1

Part One: Creation of Love 3
    The Most Beautiful Thing in this World 5
    Life 7
    Story Time 9
    Clouds 11
    The Best in Me 13
    Just a Touch 15
    Seasons 17
    Love Was Meant to be Shared 19
    I Wrote Myself a Letter 21
    Today 23
    Take Me by My Hand 25
    The Rain 27
    Candy Land 29

Part Two: Comfort Behind the Scars 31
    If A City Could Talk, Oh the Stories it Would Tell 33
    Sweet Lies 35
    I Cheated Myself 37
    The Silent Cry 39
    Pain 41
    Scars 43
    One's Mind 45

No One Understands 47
If I Were an Eraser 49
Drugs 51
Incarceration 55

Part Three: It's only Temporary 57
Life and Death 59
I Wish It Was a Dream 61
Don't Weep for Me 63
Don't Worry, Be Happy 65
Sisterly Love 67
Touch Down 69

Endorsements For The Reflection of Life 71

About the Author 77

Introduction

Reflection of Life is as if you're taking a look in the mirror. You see what others see and what they do not see.

As I thought deeply of what life has brought about, and will bring, I decided to express it all on paper. I pray that someone is inspired, encouraged, and finds healing through the gratitude of my heart.

All were written through feelings of love, release, and deliverance. When one's mind is healed then one's body is free. You are no longer bound.

Part One: Creation of Love

The Most Beautiful Thing in this World

The most beautiful thing in this world is God's creation
God created everything the way he wanted it to be

God said… Let there be light and there was light
Light was divided from the dark

The light was called day. and the darkness was called night
This was the first day, and everything started out alright

The second day the sky and water were set in motion
While on the third day came the Earth and ocean

On the fourth day, the sun, moon, and stars appeared
And that truly made everything so bright and clear

The fifth day consisted of the fish and birds
While on the sixth day, animals filled the Earth
Man and Woman were designed in creation to take care of what God was making

On the seventh day, God rested from all His work
Everything was completed, that is all that was needed

Handsome kings, and beautiful queens came out of God's creation; Everything was already set in orderly preparation

God has a plan and a purpose for each person's life
We should enjoy every moment and not spend it in strife

He even numbered our days while we are here on Earth
Therefore, live your life the best way you know how
And take life for what it is worth

Life

Life is full of surprises
One day you are happy, the next day you are sad
One minute you are smiling
The next minute you are mad

It would not be considered life if the bitter did not
go with the sweet

All of it is a learning experience
We all go through different trials and tribulations....
That is what makes us unique

No matter what life holds for us, one thing I know
to be true; God will not put any more on you than you can
bare. If he allows you to walk in it, He will see you through

Story Time

Each of us has a story that has already been written
A story that someone is sitting and ready to hear

It does not have to be lengthy
Therefore, let's make that very clear

It does one's heart justice to simply release what is inside
Because the inside is dark and gloomy, filled with pain and misery and wanting to be set free.
While the outside portrays an image that no one knows but you and me

Who do I tell my story to?
Who really cares enough to hear?

Will it be someone who is far away?
Will it be someone who is nearby?

Either or neither nor, we all have a story to tell
So, whomever I choose to tell it to….Is
Still a question waiting for me to exhale

Clouds

Clouds are an essential part of the water cycle
If we don't have clouds, we have no rain, ice, or snow
And there definitely would be no rainbow

We actually need the clouds in the sky to survive
Clouds play a major role in keeping us alive

Clouds can block light and heat from the sun
At night, clouds can also keep us warm

There may be some cloudy days in the sky
There will always be some cloudy days in your life

Have no fear
Eventually the clouds will move
And the sun will shine again
Just as bright as it was before

Also, the next time you look and see clouds in the sky
It is a reminder how important the clouds are as you are passing by

Marvin Sapp recorded a song that states, "He saw the best in me, when everyone else around could only see the worst in me." His song inspired my poem.

The Best in Me

No matter what people see, always strive
To be the best person you can be

At times people see what they choose to see
However, I can only give you who or what is inside of me

The flaws I have come with some good and bad
It is the growth in me which makes me feel glad.

I live my life to please the Lord first and then myself
Anything else falls under that statement, including whatever is left

I have been set free and whomever the Son sets free is free indeed

With that being said, I can only give you the best in me even though you still choose to see what you want to see

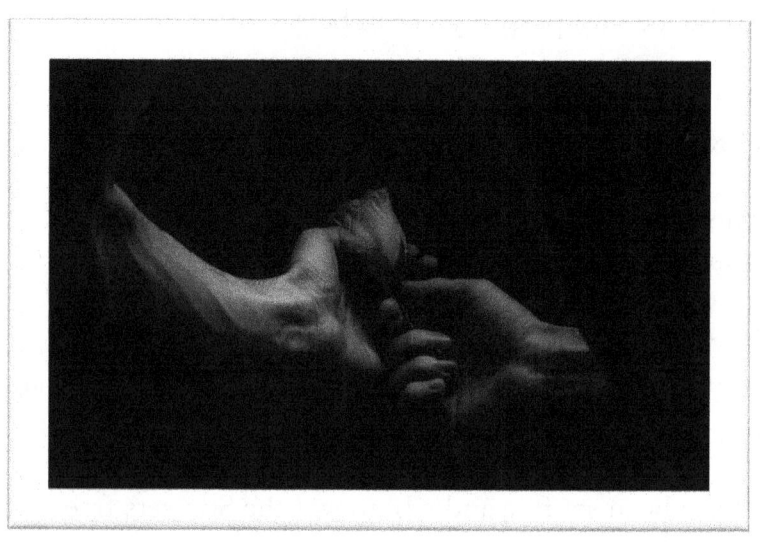

Just a Touch

All I need is just a simple touch
I don't think that is asking too much

Send me a touch of love with lots of hugs
A touch of peace and a touch of joy is all I need

Please wrap it up in a gift bag as a surprise just for me

It's the little things that put a smile on my face
Because generosity definitely goes a long way

We know emotions don't have a price on them
And true love cannot be bought

The only thing I crave is just a simple touch
From you who is constantly in my thoughts

Seasons

To everything there is a season
And to every season, there is a reason

Winter brings the cold and snow
While spring is the time to plant flowers and watch them grow

In summer, it reaches almost 100 degrees
Autumn brings the falling of leaves

Then the seasons start back over again
However, we can never predict how they will end

I have seen big drops of hail fall in the summer
I have even experienced hot days in the winter

Nevertheless, to everything there is a season
And to every season, there is a reason
We may never know the reason for the season

But what we do know is seasons have a role to play. Seasons are included in God's creation and that is definitely enough Revelation

I LOVE YOU

Love Was Meant to be Shared

Love is an intense feeling of deep affection

However, it does not mean everything will always be in perfection

Spiritually, one is perfected in the righteousness of Jesus Christ

Therefore, to understand the meaning of love goes deeper than one could imagine

However, love is expressed it is for one to hold on and keep

Love even feels good while you are fast asleep
Just to think of the passion of love is so meek

Love was meant to be shared especially to the ones who cares

Love is sincere
Love is kind
At times, love can also have you blind

It is very important to wait patiently for love
So, the love you give will also be the same love you receive

Without doubting and without questioning
It will be all the love you need

I Wrote Myself a Letter

I wrote a letter to myself
I said, Dear Self…. Take care of yourself please

Who loves you more than you?
They say self-love is the best love
I definitely found this to be true

My letter was expressed in genuine emotions
I even sprinkled it with a little perfume
I covered the letter with lots of hearts
Until I almost ran out of room.

My letter was so captivating I fell deeply in love with myself

I put all my thoughts on paper until I did not have anything left

After telling myself how I really felt, I had to bring my letter to an end

I thought of something else I wanted to say
However, when I began to start, there was no ink in my pen

I sealed my letter with lots of kisses
And dropped it in the mailbox today
I cannot wait until the mailman comes
Only, to see what the letter to myself has to say

Today

I packed my suitcase on today
I have decided to throw everything in it away

My suitcase was very heavy as you already know
Everything in it including the suitcase
Needed to be thrown slam out the front door.

My suitcase was filled with unforgiveness
Which we know forgiveness is a must
Keeping it around too long was making me lose trust

Bad memories of my past experiences were tucked deep inside
That is something I knew I definitely had to override

Other dark things would not allow my suitcase to close nor zip
I tried and tried but it was so heavy it almost began to rip

Then I finally realized I had to throw the whole suitcase away
That is when my life started back over on that special day

Take Me by My Hand

Could someone please take me by the hand and walk with me?
Lead me, guide me along the way

This journey gets difficult sometimes
The road seems so very long
Through it all, I constantly remind myself that
I must remain strong

Stumbling blocks and stones are placed in my path
If I go around, I know they will not last

This race is not given to the swift but he that shall endure until the end

Take me by the hand and don't ever let me go
I will reach my destination sooner or later
Even if I must walk slow

The Rain

When I was young, I enjoyed playing in the rain
I didn't know any better because I thought rain was God's tears falling from the sky

I didn't know then, however I do know now
God has no need to cry

Heaven is filled with pure, holiness, and righteousness which does not include tears
I guess it is a part of growing up, learning throughout the years

Now that I am older, I do not enjoy going out in the rain
But I do enjoy hearing raindrops against my windowpane

The sound of the rain and the cool air it brings allows me to rest peacefully all night

Waking up another day, only to see the precious and bright daylight, with no rain in sight

Candy Land

Welcome to the world of Candy Land which consists of nothing but sweets

Once you enter that land, you will feel as if you are on a retreat

There are chocolate bars, Hershey kisses and even lollipops

Walk a little further, you will also see some really big gum drops

Candy Land is like a dream come true; it is simply hard to believe

You don't know where to begin, and you definitely don't know where to end

Even though the land is filled with sweets, it still has a mixture of sweet and sour

There are sweet and sour patch kids, jolly ranchers, and good ole' sweet tarts

You chew and eat
You eat and chew until it all falls apart

Candy Land never closes
Therefore, you can stay all night

That may not be a good idea knowing you will chew everything in sight

As you look on the other side, you see bunches of cotton candy that looks so soft, fluffy, and sweet
You finally decide to lie down to relax your mind, on a batch of cotton candy and the next thing you know you are fast asleep.

You wake up in the morning to see it was only a dream because you are lying in your bed

Only wishing the world of Candy Land really existed while sugar plums still danced in your head

Part Two: Comfort Behind the Scars

If A City Could Talk, Oh the Stories it Would Tell

If a city could talk, oh the stories it would tell
It would tell on you
It would tell on me
It would also tell on whomever sits under the tree

The city would tell the good
The city would tell the bad
The city would also have the whole city mad

The city would tell whatever was done in the day
The city would tell what is done at night
The city would especially tell what happened when everyone was out of sight

Aren't you happy the city is unable to talk?
Because if it could, the majority of people would be at fault

What was hidden would not be a secret anymore
Remember the city saw you behind closed doors

If a city could talk, oh the stories it would tell
Whatever the city would say, oh it would definitely sell

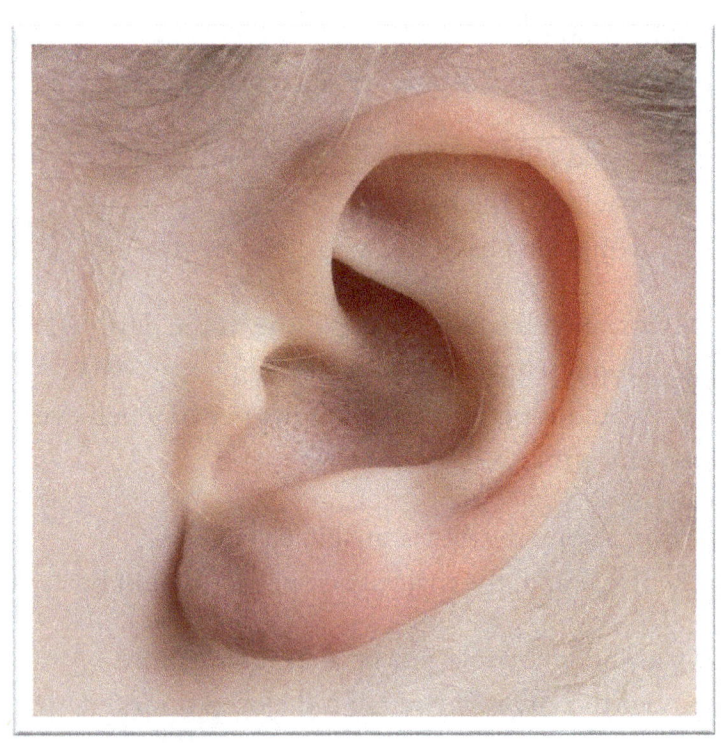

Sweet Lies

I hear the whispers of sweet lies clearly in my ear
It sounds so romantic however the love is not sincere

Your actions should have shown me that your sweet lies are not true

With the love of blindness in my eyes, I really had no clue

The whispers of sweet lies were ringing in my ear day in and day out

Until I believed every word without a shadow of a doubt

One day, I became strong till the whispers of sweet lies didn't sound so sweet anymore
This is when I decided it was time to close the whispers of sweet lies door

What a Friend we have in Jesus

I Cheated Myself

When I think of the times, I cheated myself, it turns my stomach sour

Not only did I cheat myself minute by minute but also by the hour

I cheated myself out of the life God had planned and the purpose for me to have

One day I realized you must get out of darkness because of God's grace and his mercy has sustaining power

His love will overshadow you just like no other
His love is even sweeter than that of one's mother

I cheated myself once, however I will not do it again

Because I gained real love when I found that I have a true friend

The Silent Cry

It is easy to put on a smile
It is a joy to laugh
But what happens at night when you are alone and start to feel sad?

That's when the silent cry hits because you are all alone shut in behind closed doors

Next thing you know, the tears start flowing and the sniffling of your nose

You try your best to be strong because you are all alone.
It seems as though what little strength you thought you had is truly all gone

Now it is right back to the beginning of being alone with the silent cry, which seems to not have an ending

Only you can hear it and see the tears shed
It worsens at night when you are in the bed

A silent cry can be considered dangerous because no one is aware of what you are going through

Therefore, seek to find someone trustworthy to silently cry with and share what is troubling you

Pain

Pain is hidden in one's heart
Some people will share it while others will not
Everyone has or will experience pain; therefore, the word pain still remains the same

How one handles pain solely depends on the individual

Some cry
Some release
While some just don't know where to begin
However, it goes, it is still pain and it starts deeply within

The thought of the word pain even hurts to hear
Especially when it is continuously ringing in your ear

The good thing is one day your mind will be clear and you will be set free

It may take a little time because it took a little time for me

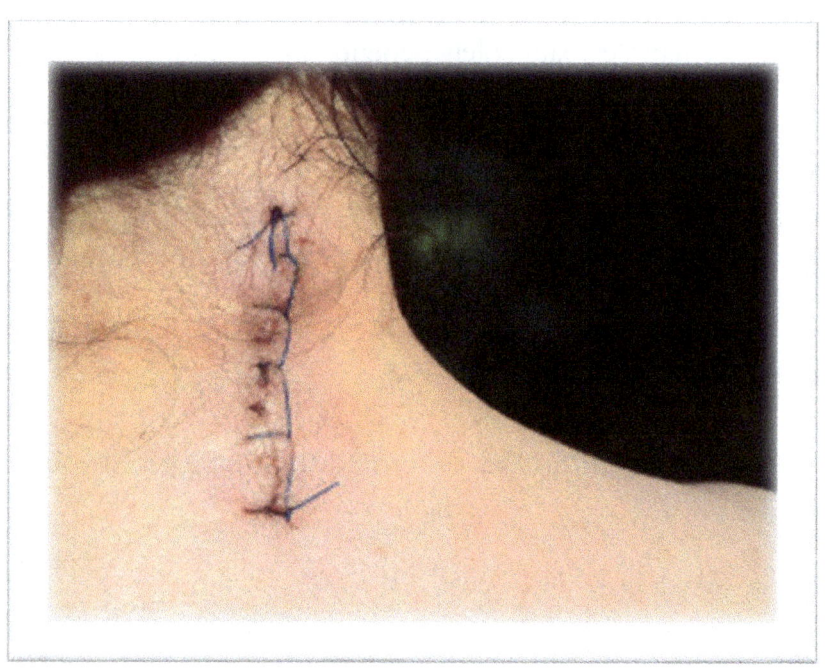

Scars

For every scar one has, there's always a testimony behind it

Some scars are little, some are big
Some are visible, some are hidden

Scars are a part of life which definitely needs time to heal
The more you comfort your scars, the more you take care of your scars

Eventually, it will become not such a big deal

The healing process is completed
The hurt and pain is no longer there
The scars are gone but there's a testimony behind it
Waiting for you to share

One's Mind

If your mind is sick, your body can not heal
This may sound as if it is just a joke, but oh no….it is real

Everything starts in the mind, which has an effect on one's body and soul

Some people's minds collect way more than it actually can hold

Your mind tells you when your body needs to rest
Listen to your mind and stop putting it through a test
It certainly knows what is best

When one's mind is clear, one can surely think
Remember
A mind is a terrible thing to waste.
It could disappear before you even blink.

No One Understands

What is the use of explaining when no one understands?
Your words come out loud and clear

However, comprehension seems as though it is not even near

I know you hear me…but are you really listening to what I have to say?

I tried so hard to explain myself
However, confusion seems to get in the way

No one understands the depth of what you have been through

I am sure there's someone out there who should be able to relate

I guess I will just get my pen and paper to write until someone is able to communicate

If I Were an Eraser

If I were an eraser, I would erase all the mistakes I ever made in life

I would erase some people; I would erase some places
I would also erase some things
I would even erase thoughts which bad memories bring

It is amazing what an eraser can do
It even can erase those things people said that were not even true

I would erase so much until there was nothing else left
Then I would go on vacation and finally relax myself

Knowingly whatever is erased is completely gone and thought of no more

Now, the rest of the erasers can be collected and placed back in the drawer

Say No to Drugs!

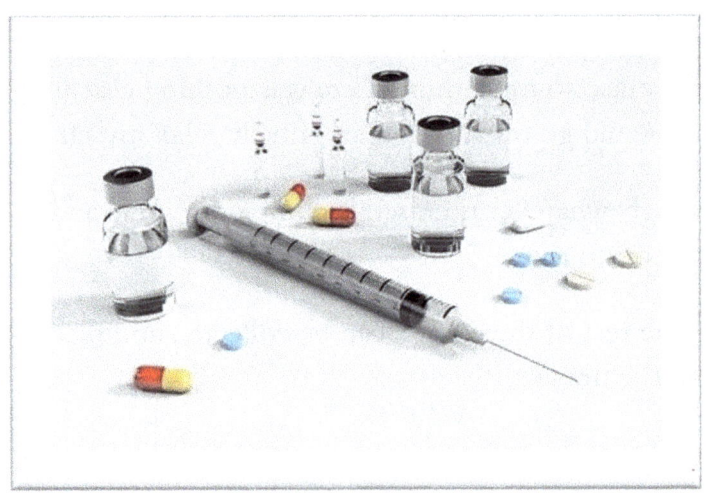

Drugs

Who ever invented harsh drugs really created the devil's playground?

Drugs have no respect of persons
It does not matter who is around

Drugs do not come to play
It is an addiction, which makes you stay
That carries you further in a dangerous way

Drugs come for girls, boys, women, and men
Don't get it twisted….
Drugs are your enemy
They are not your friend

Drugs can make you quit school
The devil will trick you to thinking it is cool
Only to laugh at you because he knows you are really acting like a fool

Drugs can have you put out of your house
Drugs can even make you lose your spouse

Drugs can take away your good looks
And make you become a lying crook

The enemy will have you thinking… Hmmm

I will only do a little and then let it go
That simply is not possible
So please, just say NO!

Don't allow the devil's seed to be planted in your life
Because it will grow
Then the next thing you know
You have no control over your own mind

While the devil sits back and mocks
Because he is working around the clock

Trying to steal, kill and destroy…
A life that you are trying to enjoy

The only thing he has on his mind is destruction
Please, do not enter the devil's playground
He will try his best to tempt you…
Especially when no one is around

Reflection of Life

Dr. Joyce F. Pullen

Incarceration

When I was incarcerated, my rights were taken away
What a miserable feeling when I was told Raleigh Correctional Center, would be my home from that day

My kids were sad because their mom was gone
Wishing that I could come back home

When I entered through those gates
That is when the prison of my mind would not allow me to escape

My life was in the hands of people dressed in blue
I used to look around and think.... This cannot be true

I was told when to get up and when to go to sleep
I was even told when to shower and also when to eat

Freedom was nowhere in sight
I was controlled by men both day and night

I was later transferred to Fountain Correction Center where I worked on the road squad making 40 cent a day

Oh me, oh my, is all I could think and all I could say
It is the price you pay for breaking the law
Prison bars and control is all that I saw

I was given a release date and finally my sentence came to an end; I was so happy to know I would be going home once again

I was released and left that prison mentality behind.

It is a testimony though because I once was bound but now, I am free

I did not allow incarceration to get the best of me
It taught me lessons that I had to learn
Giving up your freedom is not something you want to yearn

Part Three:
It's only Temporary

Please pause for a
moment of silence
for those who have gone before us

Life and Death

We talk a lot about life, but we don't talk enough about death
When in actuality the two go together within themselves

First there is life
Then there is death
Nevertheless, that is not the only thing left

We celebrate special occasions as much as we can
Not realizing death is right at hand

Life and death are like a jigsaw puzzle
You fit the pieces where they may go one after another

You are here one day and the next day you can be gone,
Get right church….Get right people before God calls you home

No judgment here, judge not that ye be not judged
I don't know where you will be

What I do know is…. there's a mansion in heaven waiting for me

Travis M. Hilliard
11/10/1983 – 3/30/2013

I Wish It Was a Dream

When I think about the horrible night, it feels only as a dream; It is as if I hear your voice saying… Mom don't worry…things are not as bad as they seem

I hate I had to leave you, but you knew I could not stay
My work on this Earth was already completed
Therefore, I had to get out of the way

I did not live to become an old man, as some elderly men do
But the life that I have lived I truly enjoyed, and it still remains to be true

I know you really miss me, and it makes you feel bad at times
However, when you start to feel sad, and it makes you want to cry, just think of the times I made you smile…Even before I said my last goodbye

Celebration of Life
Issac James Hilliard Jr.
9/30/1959 - 03/03/2001

Don't Weep for Me

Even though I have gone away
Memories of me are here to stay

I thought it was best for everyone
To show you all slowly my deed was done

There is no need to cry because it will cause pain
Just think of the good times and let that remain

I was not perfect and did not intend to be
I enjoyed my life day to day and just tried to be me

So, to my dearest family, please do not sit around and weep…but do acknowledge that it was my precious time to sleep

Dedicated to the late
McAnthony Hillard
2/16/1962 - 11/26/2011

Don't Worry, Be Happy

This is a poem that I wrote
You might want to read it note by note
But don't worry, be happy

When life throws you a lemon
Catch it and make lemonade

When life throws you some sugar, catch it
And make you some Kool-Aid

Life threw me death, I caught it
And made me a bed to lie in but don't worry, be happy

You all know how I lived my life
I worked hard and was a giving person
I also drank, partied till the break of dawn

And God knows I told a lot of lies
Which brought nothing but tears to my eyes

However, don't let what I am about to say shock you guys
It is not how I started my life out that I am proud of,
But it's how my life ended

I dedicated my life back to God
God gave me another chance to get it right, and I did
So do not worry, be happy because I am resting in peace for now

In Memory of
Constance P. Barnes
1/10/1957- 1/31/2018

Sisterly Love

A sister's love is like no other
Sometimes she takes the place of your own mother

A sister really cares about how you feel
No matter what comes your way, a sister always keeps it real

Sisters cook, clean and be there for each other
A sister's love should never depart
As a matter of fact, it should go further

When in need, a sister is always there
It doesn't matter what, it doesn't matter where

They say a sister comes from blood
To me a sister is whoever shows love

It is good to have a sister you can depend on
To be there for each other until God calls one of you home

In Honor of
Donald L. Hilliard
05/23/1969 - 09/13/2021

Touch Down

My baby brother's favorite football team was the
Dallas Cowboys

He passed that down to us
Whenever the Cowboys played, it would always be a fuss

We would scream so loud especially if they scored a touchdown
It seemed as if everyone watched football all over town

Win or lose, the Dallas Cowboys still remained my brother's favorite

He had the Cowboys jersey, hat, coat, and anything else that he could find
Cowboys, Cowboys, and more Cowboys was all on my brother's mind

One day my brother's health declined, and the ball was thrown to him

After years and years of being a Cowboy's fan, he finally got his chance to play

He ran and ran until no one could catch Him
And finally, he scored his touchdown…
What a loud scream of joy in heaven it was on that day

Reflection of Life

Dr. Joyce F. Pullen

Endorsements For The Reflection of Life

Dr. Joyce Pullen is a true inspiration to everyone she encounters. She is not one who hides her past. She uses her past to be a testimony to others. She lets you know that with God, strength, and determination, you can overcome anything.

Although she has faced many losses, trials and tribulations, Dr. Pullen continues to be a God-fearing, loving, courageous, and giving soul. If she has one, you know you have half. Through friendship, outreach and ministry, Dr. Pullen has been and continues to be a blessing to so many in her community and surrounding areas.

She is now sharing her gifts and talents through her artistry of poetry. Her work will touch your heart, your soul and even your funny bone. She is a straight shooter who tells it like it is. Sometimes, the words may seem a little brash, but they are all out of love. The truth is not to be sugar coated, it is to be delivered directly and that is exactly what she does.

With kindness and love in her heart, she is going to give you what you need to hear, not necessarily what you want to hear. That is the true definition of a Christian Friend. That is the true definition of Dr. Joyce F. Pullen.

Submitted by: Sharon High-Jones

Dr. Joyce Faye Pullen, affectionately known to me as Faye, you had a dream and goal in mind of becoming an author of this great book and you have succeeded. I have watched you accomplish your goals one by one and I am excited to read this book.

As your best friend, I know that whatever you put your mind to, you succeed with excellence. This book is going to be a phenomenal work coming from you Dr. Pullen. As a woman of God, I applaud you. I love you Queen and continue to be great on all your endeavors.

    Your childhood friend, Felecia (Lisa) Boyette

Revelation 2:19 *reads* "I know your deeds, your love and faith, your service and perseverance, and that you are now doing more than you did at first." Joyce has endured in her service to the Lord, her perseverance in helping ALL people in her service to God.

Her loving service is known to God for all things like Christ. This book is a testimony of her life in Christ. Her ministry is a way to demonstrate the empowerment of God's love in her heart.

It is my hope that her words help you gain a vision of the love and self-worth that you will find to empower your walk in God's walk as you see here in Joyce. She has been a devout blessing to me and my life. I aim to be more like Christ Jesus, Amen.

Written in Love by,
Elder Lori Hines Jones, MPA

I have known Pastor Pullen, whom I affectionately call "Faye" or "Mom" since the early 1980's. Her nurturing and kind spirit is what drew me to her and it is one of the traits that have kept us connected.

She is a mighty woman of God who speaks her mind and is always advocating for those who may not feel they have the strength to do so. If she sees that you are being used or mistreated, she brings it to your attention and equips you with the courage to get through any situation.

She works hard to make others feel loved, have a smile on their face and feel encouraged that good things are waiting for them. She has an amazing personality: she is the kind of friend you always want to have in your corner.

I love my dear friend. She is a Queen who has so much in store for her.

Submitted by: Wanda Best

About the Author

Dr. Joyce F. Pullen is an Outreach Pastor who enjoys helping people. She oversees God's Gift of Ministries in Different Recoveries (GGOM), LLC.

Dr. Pullen received a diploma in biblical studies-Course One in September 2002 and Course Two in September 2003 from the Wilson Chapel United Free Will Baptist Church through the Higher Learning Bible Institute.

In 2018, Dr. Pullen received her Doctor of Theology Degree from Manna Bible College in Wilson, North Carolina.

She was also awarded the Black History Community Service Award from the Manna Bible College Alumni Association.

Dr. Pullen works tirelessly throughout the streets in the community. Some of her detailed outreach includes street witnessing, clothing, food, and gift bag give-aways. She also hosts annual coat drives. Her mission work includes visiting the sick-n-shut in, nursing homes and hospitals.

Her motto is "It Could have been Me."

In her leisure time, she enjoys the simplicities of life. She is a firm believer in the phrases "Keep it Real" and "Your Word is Your Bond."

Always remember, "When you are blessed by the best, there's no need to be stressed."

Contact Information:
Facebook: Joyce Pullen
Email: pullenjoyce71@gmail.com

His Glory Creations Publishing, LLC is an International Christian Book Publishing Company, which helps launch and the creative works of new, aspiring, and seasoned authors across the globe, through stories that are inspirational, empowering, life-changing, or educational in nature, including poetry, children's books, journals fiction and non-fiction.

DESIRE TO KNOW MORE?

Contact Information:
CEO/Founder: Felicia C. Lucas
Website: www.hisglorycreationspublishing.com
Email: hgcpublishingllc@gmail.com
Phone: 919-679-1706

www.ingramcontent.com/pod-product-compliance
Lightning Source LLC
Chambersburg PA
CBHW051659090426
42736CB00013B/2450